DECEMBERS

Poems

MERCER
UNIVERSITY PRESS

Endowed by

TOM WATSON BROWN

and

THE WATSON-BROWN FOUNDATION, INC.

DECEMBERS

Poems

James A. Perkins

Mercer University Press
Macon, Georgia

MUP/ P477

1400 Coleman Avenue
Macon, Georgia 31207

First Edition

Books published by Mercer University Press are printed on acid-free paper that meets the requirements of the American National Standard for Information Sciences—Permanence of Paper for Printed Library Materials.

Detail of cover photo by Jack Reed, used with permission.

Mercer University Press is a member of Green Press Initiative (greenpressinitiative.org), a nonprofit organization working to help publishers and printers increase their use of recycled paper and decrease their use of fiber derived from endangered forests. This book is printed on recycled paper.

Library of Congress Cataloging-in-Publication Data

Perkins, James A., 1941-
[Poems. Selections]
Decembers : poems / by James A. Perkins. -- First edition.
pages cm
Summary: "Poems of personal memories and images of the season. The poems in Decembers have been written, usually one a year, beginning in 1973 when the author moved from the South to New Wilmington, Pennsylvania, where he took a job teaching creative writing at Westminster College. They are written to accompany the Christmas cards he and his wife Jane writes each year to keep in touch with friends from college, graduate school, and earlier jobs. These poems arise out of memory, both of the author and those of others. In them Perkins is much more interested in the images of the season, the sights, the sounds, the scents, the textures, and the tastes than he is in the abstractions: joy, love, warmth, gratitude, etc. He is more interested in what the season is than in what it means. A short story that closes the book tells of how one day Perkins saw one of his December poems on Nancy Lewis's refrigerator in Bethany, Connecticut, and wondered how many other refrigerators were so decorated. The story came out of that wondering. We all have memories of the Christmas season; they are all deeply personal and unique, and yet, curiously they are all pretty much alike. Readers will find fragments of their pasts as they read these poems. Perkins is the author of Snakes, Butterbeans, and the Discovery of Electricity"-- Provided by publisher.
ISBN 978-0-88146-465-8 (pbk. : alk. paper) -- ISBN 0-88146-465-1 (pbk. : alk. paper)
1. December--Poetry. I. Title.
PS3616.E7454D454 2013
811'.6--dc23

2013027501

for Jane
who writes the cards

and

for Nancy Lewis
whose refrigerator door inspired the story

Acknowledgments

"Bare Ruined Choirs," *Black Fly Review* 7 (spring 1986), 15.
"Breathing Form," *Black Fly Review* 10 (1989), 79.
"By the Rivers of Babylon," *Quadrangle* 1/2 (fall 1979), 5.
"The Cold is No Fiction," *U.S. 1 Worksheets* 30/31 (1995), 7.
"Cross Country Skiing," *The Cape Rock* 22/1 (spring 1987), 6.
"December Morning," *Antigonish Review* 61 (spring 1985), 83.
"Dr. Zhivago Remembers, " *Zusu's Petals Quarterly* 1/1 (winter/spring 1992), 29.
"Druid's Winter Night," *Footwork: The Paterson literary Review "89*, 36-37.
"Invisible Deaths," *Colorado Review* New Series 13/1 (fall 1985), 72.
"Lambertville Lace." *U.S. 1 worksheets* 18/19 (winter 1985), 17.
"Opening Day/Hot Stove League/1983," *Spitball* 14 (April 1985), 12.
"Oranges Were Special," *Inlet* 17 (December 1987), 17.
"Owl Cries," *Penn Power Profile* 4/4 (winter 1976), 16.
"The Specific Gravity of Fruitcake," *Poetry Center 1991 Anthology*. (Paterson, NJ: Passaic County Community College, 1991), 39.
"Stacking Wood," *Black Fly Review* 7 (spring 1986), 16-17.

Note to the Reader

If you would like to receive future poems in the *Decembers* series each year, please send your email address to jperkins@westminster.edu.

Antiphanes said merrily, that in a certain city the cold was so intense that words were congealed as soon as spoken, but after some time they thawed and became audible; so that the words spoken in winter were articulated next summer.

—Plutarch

Contents

Introduction

In the fall of 1973, my wife Jane and I left Knoxville, Tennessee, where I had completed my Ph.D. in American literature and moved to New Wilmington, Pennsylvania, where I had taken a job at Westminster College teaching English and creative writing. Since both of us were from the South, the cold and the long darkness of that first Pennsylvania winter came as a shock. That first Christmas, as Jane sat down to write cards by hand to our friends and relatives in brighter, warmer places, I wrote a poem to be enclosed with the card.

I suppose now you would have to say that was the beginning of a tradition. Now forty years later, we are still in New Wilmington. I have retired from Westminster College. It is still dark and cold in December. Jane still writes cards by hand and I work on a poem. Jane says that those poems are the only real benefit she has derived from my avocation. Early on, we both learned there was no money in poetry, but we learned there was no poetry in money either.

These then are the December poems. They are by no means all of those that I have written. Sometimes when the cold and the dark turns me to produce a particularly twisted or bitter one, Jane says "I'm certainly not going to send that with the Christmas cards" and sends me off to try again. I have added one or two of the rejected poems, one that grew too long (and therefore too heavy and too costly) to send at Christmas, and one that was written specifically as a Christmas gift for Jane.

By the Rivers of Babylon

. . . they that carried us away
captive required of us a song. . .
—Psalm 137

Strangers in a strange land
Covered with snow
We sing on
Warmed by our memories
Of other climes
And you.

Owl Cries

Down our chimney three things have come:
Snow drifting down to die
Sizzling and spitting in the fire,
The hollow echo of Amish horses' hooves,
And once a big barn owl,
Like a phoenix risen through the flames,
Blinded by the smoke and light,
Clutching the screen with fearful talons
Till we caught him in a grocery sack.
We tossed him in the yard and watched.
He took two awkward, feathered steps,
Found the sky, and rose in graceful flight
Never asking what or who.

Dr. Zhivago Remembers

Surrounded now
By a whiter emptiness
I build a lean-to
With the over-turned sled
Of my memory
Before—
Surrendering to numbness—
I expose my throat
To the wolves.

Druid's Winter Night

Here in snow country
Under a full moon
The land lies wrapped and waiting.
Except for their mistletoe
Oaks stand naked in the wind.
Cold blues my body
As I crunch over crusted snow
To drag a fir tree home.
Inside, practicing the rune lore
Of the Winter Solstice
To keep in touch
With scattered friends,
You lay aside your pen.
The tree raised,
We stand together
Breathing in its promise,
Dreaming of Spring.

The Homecoming

> *"And oh, Aunt Em, I'm so glad to be home again!"*
> *—L. Frank Baum,* The Wizard of Oz

While a cameraman shoots
Film in our bedroom
Of a hole in the ceiling
Large enough for the fat man
To drag his bag through,
A newsman says,
"Bet you're glad
You weren't here."
"You're right," I say
Like a man who knows
He will wake up any minute
Safe in bed laughing.

Tornado dreams fade
Slowly into the pounding
Of hammers. The scents
Of Christmas waft
Through the house
Covering the smell
Of fresh paint and plaster.

Now I'm glad
We're here
Under our new roof
Waiting once more.

Changeling Child

(for Brook)

We've seen the signs before
A brighter sparkle in his eyes
A stranger music in his laugh
But this year . . .
This year's leaves
Were painted late
By elves already tired
From dying summer's skies
Czechoslovakian Blue.
Now they're busy
Designing snowflakes
For a winter
Not yet come.
...Santa asked my son
(Not the tall one –
He's out delivering papers)
To stand in as an Elf
During the Christmas rush.

Bare Ruined Choirs

Outside
Bare limbs
Dance
Through sheets of snow.
As I bare my limbs
To lie between cold sheets,
This easy imagery, friend,
Haunts my sleep.
Stripped as we are in winter,
We long, in our dying back,
To blossom forth in some new way.
(Perhaps it is the snow—
Its whiteness
Drives us
Toward a purity,
But snow
Is also cold.)
I have learned
To love you as you are.

A Shaken World

New Wilmington waits
Snow-covered
Like a miniature.
Snow fills the air
The sky presses down
Like a crystal dome.
Far away
A voice whispers:
"Rosebud,
Rosebud."

Cross-Country Skiing

Behind me, scars,
Like lines of poetry
Stretching across a wide page,
Or bands
Tying me
To a past
I've known
Been through
Left my impression on.

Far away and dim
The stars
Cast no shadows
Over this frozen land
That lies blank
Before me.

On the rhythmic scrape
Of my own invention
I ride
The unscarred body
Of fresh powder.

This motion makes
A magic possible.

December Morning

Morning light
Whispered
Through the strangeness
Frost
Left on my window
Beyond the lace
I saw the bride
Virgin
White
And cold.

Opening Day / Hot Stove League / 1983

The day of the first snow
I spent the morning
Splitting crosscuts
Of green maple
Into cord wood
For next year's fires.
My boots sucked into mud;
My arms and shoulders ached
From the maul's weight
As the lift and fall
Popped the maple open.
Then I hit the knot.
The hickory handle snapped
And sent an echo up my arms
Of bats sawed off
By inside fast balls.
I dropped the shattered handle
And headed for home
Remembering to touch all the bases.

Stacking Wood

The way to stack wood
Is by the armful.
I know a lot of them
Cut and split in the woods
Then haul a pick-up full
Toss it off and stack it
Piece by piece.

I haul the crosscuts home
And split them in the yard
Where I want the wood stack.
My way saves a lot of bending
And leaves the chips and bark
Here where I can use them
Instead of in the woods
That's so much mulch already
You don't dare drop a seed
Unless you want another tree.

Anyway, like I was saying,
The way to stack wood
Is by the armful.
I split my crosscuts
With a maul,
Pick up an armful,
And walk to the stack.

That carrying does the trick.
Those billets jounce around,
Find their place,
And make the stack solid
Like kids in a large family
Who learn to fit in and be a part.

Sticks laid one by one
Are like those second cousins
From the city
Who visit weekends
And go through drawers
To discover who you really are.
They'll find a way
To bring the stack down.

Hauling in is the same as stacking.
It should be done by the armful.
Even after a blanket of snow
Settles down the pile,
It will come up
Armful at a time
Just like it went down.
The trick is to remember where.

A pile's a one-man thing.
I hate to haul in from another's stack.
It's always letting go too late or soon
Straining your back with too much
Or sending you off with half a load.
Your own stack, if you build it right,
Gives back what you gave it
Armful for armful.
A man can't ask
For more than that.

Lambertville Lace

Hunkered beside an abandoned canal
Hard by the river
That keeps New Jersey
From being Pennsylvania,
The Lace Factory
In Lambertville
Made Towle Lace
With ten machines
On the first floor.
Last Christmas Eve,
Hung by the zero temperature
And the minus-fifty wind chill,
There was lace in every window
On the empty second floor,
A ground of ancient watery glass
Held an intricate pattern of frost
That rose in lines
Like Limerick
And filtered a strange light
Into the cold bare rooms
Above the still machines.

Invisible Deaths

During the winter
In the woods
Things happen
At night
When no one is watching.

Wind-blown branches
Snapped in the cold
Lie across the tracks
Your skis made
Yesterday.
This is the way
Trees die
Twig by twig
Branch by branch
In the cold and wind.

Remember,
You have never seen
A bird die in flight
And arc
Like a feathered stone.

Most of the dust
In your house
Is dead skin
Sloughed off
When you were not watching.

The Poet Considers Moving To Seattle

I have been nearly maddened
By the tick of rain against the glass
Of my second floor bedroom window.
It has rained thirty-one
Of the past forty days.

A kid waiting for the school bus
Stands in his yellow slicker
Like a forlorn fireplug.
Worms cover the sidewalk.
Mushroom prices have fallen.
Umbrella theft is rampant.
TV newsmen don't joke
With weathermen anymore.
The north side of everything
Is covered with moss
Including the squirrels
And my cross-country skis.

Twelve and three quarters inches of rain
A record eleven of them in November
Using Sam Lightner's rule of thumb
"One inch of rain is equal to ten inches of snow,"
I calculate roughly one hundred and thirty inches
And dream of skiing
Out of my second floor bedroom window
Into a landscape completely drowned in white.

The snarl of a saw awakens me
From my dream of skiing.
My neighbor is standing in the rain
Shaping some sturdy gopher wood.

Oranges Were Special

(for Juanita Ashbrook Perkins)

Under the hand-knit muffler and mittens
Under the new dress for her doll
Under the peppermint candy cane
Under the nickel wrapped in a scarf,
My mother found an orange
Deep in the toe of her stocking
Hung over the fireplace
On a cold Christmas morning.
Oranges were special in those days
Brought by train all the way from Florida
To a town in Ohio held hard by the winter
Against the cold gray of Lake Erie.
While her brothers Lawrence and Bill
Tore and devoured their oranges
Filling the room with the scent of citrus,
She sat and held her treasure
A golden globe in her hands
Like a small sun
From very far away.

When she could wait no longer,
She carefully peeled it,
Sectioned it and ate it
Slowly piece by piece
Crushing each section
With her tongue
Against the roof of her mouth
So the juice trickled
Down her throat
Then chewing the pulp
Seeds and all

→

Chewing never swallowing
Till it was gone
All gone

And the oil on her fingers
Made her hands smell
Like Christmas for hours.

Breathing Form

If I had been born and brought up
In an igloo and lived on whales
And not in it, about the same
Would be true.
—Dylan Thomas "A Few Words of a Kind"

North of the Arctic Circle
Snow-covered most of the year
Tundra and sea ice never thaw
A changeless earth
Like a pot lid
There is no horizon
Winds are constant
Snow fills the air
Everything is lost
In a blind white

The Eskimo tongue
Captures precise detail
There are many words for snow
Nothing is; it is becoming
Nature's forms lie hidden
Until man reveals them
One by one with words
In Eskimo the word
"To make poetry"
Is the word
"To breathe"

The Specific Gravity of Fruitcake

"What the one as big as me?"
—*Charles Dickens,* A Christmas Carol

A few weeks before Thanksgiving
My mother geared our kitchen for fruitcakes
Serious fruitcakes
Dark, dense
And heavy fruitcakes
We mailed to distant relatives

"Whatcha mailin', here, bricks?"
"Fruitcake."
"Must be good fruitcake, Weighs a ton."

Those cakes were two-man jobs
Mother measured
            chopped
                    and sifted
Daddy muscled the heavy mixture
With a wooden spoon in big stone bowls
And told us tales
About the Lexington bakery
Of his college days

The house smelled wonderful
Loaf after loaf
Fruitcake baked and cooled
Daddy reread *A Christmas Carol*
Mother cleaned the kitchen
I stared at toys
In the Sears catalogue

Later wrapped in cloth
The fruitcakes slowly soaked
In rich red wine
Like an overstuffed uncle
Sipping his brandy
After a third helping
Of mincemeat pie

Too rich to eat in chunks
We sliced the fruitcake thin
As communion wafers
And ate it slowly
Careful not to drop
A sacred crumb

Sled Poem

(for Jimbo and Brook)

Cleaning the garage
I find two sleds
Hung against the wall
Their rusted runners crushed
Long ago by the weight
Of mufflered boys
Piled high in the joy
Of their descent down hills
Which taught them better than Ovid
Shakespeare or Herodotus
That life's heart-pounding transports
Are always brief
Followed by hard climbs
And worth the effort.

The Cold Is No Fiction

Once in Kentucky
In her big chair
By the fire, my mother
Liked to read about cold
In books like *Driftwood Valley*
Where the people poured boiling water
Out a window and listened.
If it shattered two floors below
On the snow crust
They stayed in that day.

Now in Pennsylvania
Cold is no fiction.
My breath forms ice
On my moustache and beard
As I turn the corner into the wind.
"The windshield factory,"
As my son called it,
Must be well below zero.
My footsteps ring
Across the snow crust,
And I wonder if somewhere in town
A beautiful woman is pouring
Water from a steaming kettle
Out a second story window
Listening for reasons
To crawl back into bed.

A Blueprint For Christmas

After a test in high school determined
That I was not college material,
I spent three years of hard time
In the vocational track:
Print Shop, Metal Shop
Wood Shop, Mechanical Drawing.
Each December I made presents:
A pack of freshly smudged cards,
A bent wastebasket,
A warped pencil holder.
When I tried to draw up plans
For a real family Christmas,
Mr. Buck said, "Concentrate
On your isometric for that feed screw."
The teachers knew I was not
Shop material either.
But my mother accepted each gift,
Even my C's in shop, with joy.
Although she had never read them,
She followed my plans
For a real family Christmas precisely.

What I Saw Out the Window

Around the corner like a dream
Of Christmas a lighted tree
Riding its front platform
The Eastern Avenue Trolley
Came stuffed with carolers
Raising "Deck the Halls"
Above the clanging bell
To set my father down
At the Maryland Avenue stop.

He winked at the dour motorman
Who stared ahead glumly
Through the brightly lit branches
Yelled "Merry Christmas"
To the fat conductor
Who was carrying the tenor line
With his strong Irish voice
And stepped from the light of the car
Into the snow and darkness.

The bell clanged twice
And tree and song floated away
Down the tracks
Headed for the car barn
By another route.

Then my father appeared
Under the porch light
Coming out of the dark and snow
His arms loaded with gifts
Like a king from the east
Bringing us all we would ever need.

Reaching for the Star

(for Harry D. Perkins, Jr. 1927-1993)

The tree topped by a star
passed down through Mother's family
to remind us all of the greatest gift
stood in the corner covered with lights
and the delicate, old, colored orbs
both the history and the promise
of Christmas.

I was Casey, Crime Photographer
Playing with my new flash camera
Click—Click—
"Got it!
Look for it in *The Morning Express*!"
when a box behind me exploded.
Paws and ears and a long, wet, pink tongue,
a black Cocker Spaniel with a big red bow,
bowled me over.
"His name is Scalawag," my brother said.
"Take him out for a romp," said my father
handing me a long leash. "Wait," said my mother
grabbing the camera. FLASH!

She was too close, so I am a plaid blur
in my bathrobe bending over the dog
who tore around the tree
and headed for the front door.
Before anyone could say "Timber"
or "Merry Christmas" the leash toppled
the tree toward my brother

who stood, the only clear picture
from that day, in a light blue sweater,
with life stretched out before him,
reaching for the star.

The Gifts of a Roadside Magus

(for Walter Miller 1928-1994)

The men who ran the neighbor farms
when I was growing up, Kendig,
Gibson, Turner, and McBee,
were men schooled in the mysteries
of soil and seed and weather.
They knew the signs, the seasons,
the aching satisfaction of hard work,
and the slow gifts of the fruitful land.

Walter Miller knew the mysteries too.
He brought fresh vegetables from the earth
and sold them at his roadside stand,
potatoes, squash, cucumbers, peppers,
tomatoes, and most memorably, corn,
not the Shoe Peg or Golden Bantam
of my youth, but sweet new hybrids
grown with care and wonder.

After the pumpkins and cider,
as the cold came on, Walter
shuttered closed the stand,
hung a star on the silo
high above his stable,
watched the banked snow
fill his fields, and studied
the future in seed catalogs.

Walter was as close as we come,
nowadays, to a wise man.

Looking for Charles Dickens

> "[D]uring the composition of *A Christmas Carol*, [Dickens] wept and laughed and walked fifteen or twenty miles 'about the black streets of London… when all the good folks had gone to bed.'"
>
> —John Mortimer, "Introduction," *A Christmas Carol: A Facsimile Edition of the Autograph Manuscript*

From the Temple Bar in Fleet Street
through the Inns of Court
past the Old Curiosity Shop
to the Cheshire Cheese
and finally at his Doughty Street home
filled with razors, walking sticks, notebooks,
first editions, letters, watch fobs, translations,
top hats, theatre tickets, and overshoes,
we looked for Charles Dickens,
the man who invented Christmas—
Ebenezer Scrooge,
old Fezziwig, Bob Cratchit, Tiny Tim,
Jacob Marley in his chains,
and those three spirit visitors.

The great man wasn't there.
He had slipped away
wearing a mackintosh
against the gathering cold and damp
to walk the early dark
along the narrow echoing streets
between the hunched and staring houses
to the walnut fastness
of his private club.

→

We glimpsed him
near Russell Square
in the Underground
and on the upper deck
of a Marylebone bus
in the honest faces
of work-tired Londoners
heading to a neighborhood pub
for a pint of bitter.

Believing in Snowflakes

We snipped away at folded paper
then opened it to reveal
jagged snowflakes we taped
to the first grade windows
in anticipation of snow
which almost never fell
in Kentucky.

Miss Patrick told us
no two snowflakes were alike.
The ones in the windows were unique.
No two looked alike,
and not one looked like a snowflake.

Later, on the playground
I caught snowflakes on my mittens
and stared at each one till it melted.
No two looked alike, but bigger kids said
that was just something they told you
because you could never check.

A lifetime of people,
family, friends, students, and colleagues,
each wonderfully unique,
has taught me to believe
in snowflakes.

People are like that.
They can make you believe
in all kinds of things
you can never check.

The Ghost of Christmas Past

Bearing canned goods, staples
and a ham tossed in by the church elders,
our youth group roamed down hallways wrapped
in the stench of cabbage with an undertow of urine
to a room full of Cratchits
where a shamed husband stood
sullen in the shadows
while his wife, like a fecund Madonna,
six spotless children in worn clothes
moiling about her like puppies,
glowed under a single naked light bulb
hung from the ceiling.
No multitude of Heavenly Hosts,
we mangled "Joy to the World."
Our gifts declared us Magi.
"Thank you, thank you," she whispered.
We stood mute as shepherds
in the face of so much need and wondered
what they would eat in February.

A Sign

Topping church steeples
crosses of red neon
float in the night air
above Korean cityscapes.

Seen from great distances
like mountain-top flares
that flashed news
during the Chosen Dynasty,

They burn with the good news
that weary travelers
on a winter's evening
might find rest.

Pre-Millennial Snit

for Edwina Randall

Christ
he started it all
by showing up sometime
a year or two before or after
he was born.

The calendar was Julian then
and remained so until
a sixth century monk
began to tinker with time,
for the sake of God.

Gregory didn't know nothing.
When he began the count with one,
Arab traders had yet to bring "zero" to Europe.
Their other gifts, algebra and numerals,
caused me grief in high school
and kept this from being the year MCMXCIX.

In 1901, when most people who counted
knew, the 20th Century began.
This year, ignorance, popular culture, and greed
are selling our century short,
getting out early while the getting's good.

We noble few are standing firm,
Determined to be among those who count.
We wish you the best of this season
and scream like Cubs fans
at these premature millennialists:
"Wait till next year."

Trajectory

(for Harry D. Perkins, Sr. 1905-2000)

As a child, my father
had osteomyelitis, crutches,
a paper route and a shoeshine box.
His father worked for fifty cents a day.

There was never much for Christmas,
some years a tree, some years none,
no toys, nothing to play with,
clothes, usually homemade,
something useful he could wear,
a coat, trousers, gloves,
a cap, or a scarf.

Always family,
those who make it,
those close enough to come,
cousins, aunts, and uncles,
and food, always chicken,
soup beans, potatoes, fresh bread,
and pies.

At church
on the Sunday nearest Christmas,
a small bag of stick candy
and sometimes an orange.

But somehow it was enough
to create the trajectory
that has kept him "going toward"
for 95 years.

How Silently, How Silently

(for Joshua Philip and Rory Michael)

Twice now we have studied wonder
standing gape-mouthed
as star-stunned shepherds
at the edge of cries.

In the Perkins clan it's always boys.
Now there are two more
cousins so close in age
they could be twins
yet so different in style
Rory usually deep in thought
Joshua ready with a smile.

We are reacquainted with small:
fingers, ears, toes, and noses,
And with beginnings:
cooing, reaching, rolling, crawling, and standing
bright-eyed and poised on the edge of possibility.

We love them both
and celebrate their health;
no matter what else the Magi bring
we have all we need.

The Gift of Language

(for my grandsons)

The cousins
Joshua, age two,
and Rory,
five months younger,
will rip open Christmas
with wonder and enthusiasm.
Bows and tissue and ribbon
will explode
in their hands
exposing toys and books
and special things for boys.

But the real gift
this year
is language.
Rory is enchanted
in a language all his own,
a gathering of sound
that is hastening to words.
Joshua has slowed sound
into syllable

and now says:
"present,
                    open,
                              mine."

Trees

Like my friend Nels Oestreich, my father
could give me a name for every tree.
He knew his field biology.
By leaf in summer and bark in winter,
he could name them all.
And he knew their uses.

"Hickory makes great handles,
oak a fine barrel;
willow can be woven well;
locust is a dense wood—
a locust post will last forever."

My father tried to teach me
about the trees, but as a teen,
I was dense as a locust post
I know the maple leaf and oak;
I tell the sycamore by its bark
and spot the Willow by its dance.

Most other trees remain a mystery.
I have one in my yard
(a Pennsylvania Ash, I'm told),
whose leaves come late and are the first to fall;
its smooth bark whispers nothing to my palm.

But, when all the other trees are bare,
One tree I know by heart—
inside or out, plastic or real,
green, pastel or white—
this tree figures forth our hope,
this Christmas tree.

A Long Path

(for Jane)

We were walking in silence
on a long drive
that twisted up a hill
toward a friend's home
for a Christmas party.
It was cold, a crisp, moonlit night.
Fresh snow clung to the trees
and covered the ground,
but the asphalt held the day's heat
and we left no tracks on the drive.

You took my glove in yours
and said, "I didn't know
it would be this long."

You shouldn't say such things to poets
in the moonlight on a snowy night.
You know how we are,
how everything becomes a metaphor
and always more than what it seems.

Suddenly I could barely walk.
I thought of other times,
of the tracks we've made,
our two sons
their fine wives
two grandsons
and more than forty years.

→

Perhaps two hundred yards up the drive,
I lightly squeezed your gloved hand
in mine and said, "I'm glad it is."
You gave me that look you use
to respond to my non sequiturs,
and we walked on in silence.

Christmas in June

Jane wants to move Christmas to June 25th.
She figures one solstice is as good as another;
she says it wouldn't be as cold
(a matter of considerable degree
here in western Pennsylvania)
and travel would be safer;
we wouldn't be stuffed from Thanksgiving;
and we'd have more time in summer
to shop and wrap and write cards.
It could be good for the poets as well.
We might have carols and hymns to rewrite.
Chances are merchants (with two quarters left
to make their year) would happily adapt.
The traditional Dickens Christmas
and Bing Crosby would still play
in the Southern hemisphere,
and we would see the magic
from a fresh perspective
in our shorts.
Cool!

Faded Angel

(for Jack Ridl)

We're cutting back this year,
no tree,
no greenery looping
down the stairs,
no display of favorite cards
from Christmases past.

With our boys far away
creating holiday memories
with their own families,
we're content with a few snowmen,
two seasonal place mats,
and candles here and there.

But one thing stays the same.
Blonde and blue-eyed,
our calico angel,
her left arm up flung
and her legs crossed
like a Scots sword dancer's,

her wings faded
from the slant light
of thirty Decembers,
still smiles her welcome
from our front door.

A Sunday Morning in Oxford

Michaelmas Term draws to a close.
College choirs present readings and carols
by candlelight in chapels
worn by the knees of believers.
Along St. Giles, the city fathers
string stars and snowflakes in trees
still fully green with leaves.
One Sunday morning in Oxford,
we walk out into the crisp cold
to find that a freezing fog
(another thing we've never seen)
has made every spider web in town
seem sugared into thick white yarn.
In a box hedge, one looks like a star
and makes me think of a stable
(no, not that one), a stable in Brooklin, Maine,
where I imagine a man named White
looks at the troubles in our time
and asks a spider to write:
"Peace On Earth."

The Illusion of Depth

Snow-covered and fog-shrouded,
the southern Ohio landscape
Is a sheet of expensive paper
toothy and off-white.

Fence posts and weeds
in the foreground
suggest an Oriental painting.

For the most part,
there is no horizon.
Occasionally a line of dark trees
pushes through the fog and snow,
like the charcoal marks
the dying Matisse
drew on his walls,
to create the illusion
of depth.

"Christmas Gift": the Ages of Man

"...and the awful responsibility of Time."
—Robert Penn Warren, All the King's Men

I am sitting now where my father sat,
in the front of the bus, remembering
how time would drag in December.
From Thanksgiving to Christmas
seemed like years. Now exams
and the end of Fall term seem to come
minutes after Spring's graduation, and I imagine
gifts no one will have to dust or move.

My sons are not sitting. They are trying
to keep ahead of things, measuring time,
from one Christmas to the next,
by hunting and gathering.
As one full week fades,
the next full week appears.
They imagine gifts to bring
wonder to their sons' eyes.

My grandsons are not sitting where my sons sat.
They are in the back in mandatory car seats.
Clearly time drags for them too.
As Fall deepens and the sun slants lower in the trees,
they loiter in toy stores,
their eyes darting and sparkling
over the vast array of this year's must-have items,
as they imagine an "opening" that will bring
them *everything*, if only it ever comes.

A Christmas Imperative with Footnotes

"Make it New!... Day by day, make it new"
— Ezra Pound Canto *53*

In this been there, done that world
where all the malls, politicians, houses,
coffee spoons,[1] and freshman themes are the same,
and everyone seems determined to become
ready-to-wear-right-off-the-rack
interchangeably everyone else,[2]
I am grateful for snow and grandchildren.

A fresh fall of snow
can flatten the light
and blur the outlines
of the most familiar landscape,
so I can stand in my own yard,
squint into the trackless waste,
and ask, "What place is this?"

Rory and Joshua
can strip the dullness from the earth
with the same speed and energy
they rip into presents,
when they stop, suddenly quiet,
point at something I walk by everyday,
and say, "Look, Poppa!"

---

[1] "I have measured out my life with coffee spoons" is a line from T.S. Eliot's "The Love Song of J. Alfred Prufrock" published in *Prufrock* in 1917.

[2] This line came from a talk delivered to the faculty of Maryville College on May 16, 1979 and later reprinted as an article "51 Ford or College" in *Quadrangle* (Spring, 1979). It was suggested by the sentence "The very thought of being oneself in a epoch of interchangeable selves must appear supremely ridiculous" in "nonlecture two" from e.e. cummings *Six Nonlectures* 1953.

Old School Christmas

This Christmas will be "old school."
After thirty-two years at one address,
we moved, last summer, to a two-floor apartment
in the old New Wilmington Elementary School.
the downstairs carved out of Brook's kindergarten
and the upstairs out of Jimbo's sixth grade classroom.
I expect to awaken
to cut-paper snowflakes
in all the windows
construction paper garlands
red and green swags
hanging from all the walls,
the smell of rubber boots,
wet wool, library paste
and the excitement
of generations of children
who knew that Christmas
was really about anticipation.

Food & Tradition

For most of us the holidays
are a blend of food and tradition,
favorite recipes that stir memories
and teach children the family lore.

For Jane, it's her mother's chilled fresh ambrosia,
whole, black, pitted olives
and sandwiches of left-over turkey
slathered with Durkee's Famous Sauce.

For me, it's escalloped oysters.
My mother made them every year,
beside the turkey at Thanksgiving,
beside the ham at Christmas.

This year we will make them again
from a recipe in *Kentucky Monthly*:
butter,
crackers (both butter & saltine),
oysters
heavy cream
and a sprinkle of black pepper

layered in a casserole
and baked for half an hour.

When I spoon the briny, slick, buttery richness
onto my plate, after fifty years, I will be
home for the holidays.

Shagbark Hickory Nuts

"Later on in the program we will be having a talk from Gertrude Hazelette entitled 'The Superior Way to Crack Hickory Nuts.'"
—Fannie Flagg *Standing in the Rainbow*

Each year during the holidays
my mother filled the cherry nut bowl
Uncle Lawrence carved from a solid block
with store-bought nuts:
almonds
filberts or hazel nuts
Brazil nuts
pecans
and English walnuts.
We ate them from Thanksgiving to Christmas.

Then on Christmas day we'd open a box
of Georgia paper-shell pecans
sent by Miss Shuff, a first grade teacher
at my father's school. You could crack them
with your fingers.

From the early fall till Thanksgiving
and after the holiday nuts were gone,
all we had were shagbark hickory nuts
from the three big trees on the back corner
of the farm. They were small and thick hulled.
You had to work hard with both cracker and picks
to get at bits and slivers of nut meat.
But when you spread them
over a glazed rolled pork loin,
they created a taste you remember
forever.

Ways of Looking at Thirteen Snowmen

The Amish typically accept the photographing of their way of life, but they forbid photos of themselves because they believe such things are graven images in violation of the Second Commandment. (For this same reason, the dolls of young Amish girls are traditionally faceless.)
www.religionfacts.com

I

At sundown on Tuesday,
thirteen snowmen, created
during lunch, stand
in front of the Amish school
on Poverty Point road
in the single digit cold

II

Thirteen gentleman callers
dressed for the prom
in white dinner jackets

III

Coal from the scuttle
for mouths and eyes
carrots from lunch boxes
for noses
give the snowmen
personalities as individual
as their creators

IV

A chain of snowmen cut from folded paper

V

Footprints of all sizes
surround the snowmen;
shouts, laughter and visible breath
still hang above the ringing crusted snow

VI *The Thirteen Most Beautiful Boys*
from Andy Warhol's "Screen Tests" (1964)

VII A little girl holds up a doll
to let her feel the features
of the snowman's face

VIII Snow-shrouded Terracotta Warriors
a long march from Xi'an,
the mountain passes to the south
blocked by heavy snows,
turn their faces to the north
and assume this must be Mongolia

IX The snowmen smell
denim steaming dry
near the school's stove
after lunch

X The Da Vinci Cold:
"The Last Supper," alfresco
in the sub-zero wind chill

XI A shiver of actors auditioning
for the lead in "The Burl Ives Story."

XII Stranded Radio City Music Hall Rockettes,
their bus having died, await rescue
in long eider-down coats and Uggs®

XIII When Frank Parrish
of the *Globe-Leader*
aims his camera
they try
to turn their faces
away.

The Importance of Boxes

We're not packrats
or environmentalist crazies.
At what Brook once called the "opening,"
on Christmas morning, we don't save
wrapping paper, carefully removed
and flattened out, for future use.
We throw ribbon and bows
into a black trash bag as we go.

But we do save boxes,
boxes from stores
that no longer exist:
Pogue's, Coppin's, McRae's
Shillito's, Kennington's, Horne's
Rollman's, Strouss's, and Troutman's.
Stores we shopped in
before there was only Macy's and Dillard's.

These vintage boxes
are as sure a link
to Christmas Past
as Dickens's first ghost.

I remember how Jimbo
would dump out all his toys
and sit for hours
in the empty cardboard box.
He knew.

The dress shirt and tie
I open may have come from Macy's
but what I treasure is the Woody's box
that I will save and wrap
for someone else next year.

Christmas Lights

When I was too young to worry about German bombers
targeting the machine-tool plants of Cincinnati,
my uncle crafted gliders at the Baldwin Piano factory
while my father, a block warden, patrolled every night
to maintain the total darkness of blackouts.
But in our front room behind heavy curtains
my father hung strings of colored lights
on our Christmas tree in mid December.
If one bulb burned out the whole string went dark
and we had to check each bulb to find the faulty one.
"It's a series circuit son. They all depend on each other."
Three months after VJ Day, when Mrs. Molique threw butterbeans
all over our back yard, our neighbors outlined their houses
in Christmas lights because they could. I wanted to do ours
so Santa could find us, but mother said,
"It's not our way, son, to call attention to ourselves."

Kodak Jelly Roll Pan

Jane makes sausage balls for Christmas
following a recipe she no longer even reads
in the *Central Presbyterian Church Cookbook*.
They are Brook's favorite snack.
I've slowed down on them since the bypass.
The thing I like best about them
is the baking sheet she uses,
an aluminum jelly roll pan,
seventeen and a half by twelve
with a one inch lip, that looks
as if the French army marched over it
during their retreat from Moscow.
It wasn't the French army. It was Jimbo
using it as a sled one cold December day
on the small steep embankment
behind P building in Golf Range
our first year in Knoxville.
Just looking at that pan,
as Jane slides the sausage balls off,
is better than watching a home movie.

The All-American, Coast to Coast, Icebox Poetry Anthology

1. Background

When I was young—young enough to waste a few dollars each year on the Yale Younger PoetsAward contest—I gained a certain notoriety as a poet when I became known throughout the publishing world as "The Man Who Kills Magazines." That is old news; I confessed all that years ago in *Story Quarterly* (those of you who are compelled to do that sort of thing can look it all up in volume 7/8 [1978]: 40-43), and I have lived quite happily in the years since, extorting about $1000 a month from America's little and literary magazines by writing simple business letters in the privacy of my own home. Here is an example of one of the letters.

> Dear Editor,
>
> If you don't send me a check for $1000 by return mail (see my S.A.S.E. enclosed), I will submit some poetry to your magazine.
>
> Sincerely,
> James A. Perkins
> "The Man Who Kills Magazines"

How about that!

2. The Problem

As I said earlier, it has been a pleasant enough life with the poetry money coming in regularly to supplement what I make teaching English at a small, liberal arts college in Western Pennsylvania, but now I want more. I want to put out my "collected poems." I'm mature enough. I've paid my dues. I've been at it long enough. Even though I have only published a few of my poems in magazines (this was early on and in the very last issue of each of those magazines), I have kept writing steadily for the past thirty-four years. A check of my carefully kept poetry journals shows that, to date, I have written 871 poems.

Recently I sent a 97-page manuscript to a university press. The editor returned it almost immediately with this note.

> Dear James Perkins:
>
> Although your poems are strong, vivid and, in many ways, quite moving, we generally prefer to publish an author's "collected works" only after that author has established himself (and a potential market for his works) by publishing a large number of individual poems in little and literary magazines. I have enclosed a listing of the magazines we here at the press consider among the very best now publishing poetry.
> Sincerely,
>
> Natu Brave, Editor

Indeed enclosed was a list of magazines almost identical to the list I had used over the years to supplement my income.

The problem appeared to be that I couldn't get my "collected works" published until I could prove that there was an audience for my poetry by having it published in magazines, and if I sent a poem to a magazine, it died.

3. Alternative Publishing

It wasn't as if there weren't an audience for my poetry. I have been sending my work to friends and acquaintances these past thirty-four years. At first I just sent a seasonal poem along with the Christmas cards my wife carefully and personally wrote each year. Then I got so I would pull a batch of recent poems together and send them off to anyone whose critical opinion I respected. Beginning in the late 80's, I faxed poems all over the globe. Now I attach my poems to e-mail and zip them off at the speed of light.

4. Critical Response

People like my poems. I know they do. I have proof. In the beginning, I would get critical responses (a year later) in Christmas cards: "We really enjoyed Jim's poem about whatever it was; we are looking forward to this year's." Then later, I got an occasional letter commenting on the poems: "Lots of `blood' & `death' & `love' in these poems. You must be trying to hang on to your southern roots." Then faxes: "Got the poems thru pg. 8; then the FAX ran out of paper." And finally e-mail: "Do you think writing on these machines has changed your poetry in any way?" Well, to be quite honest, when you pull it altogether, this does not really add up to a ringing recommendation of my work. I do have one, however. Iceboxes.

5. Iceboxes

My wife says that they are called refrigerators, that they have been called refrigerators since before I was born, and that my calling them iceboxes is as retarded as my obsession for trolley cars. I love trolley cars, but this is about poetry.

Anyway, a few years ago at a party thrown by a new member of the political science department, I was headed for another beer when I noticed something on the icebox door, one of my poems, a faint photocopy of a faxed original, held there by two fruit-shaped magnets. I suppose I could have said, "Where did you get this poem?" But I barely knew the guy through his wife who was teaching a couple of freshman composition courses for the department as an adjunct instructor, so I let it drop. Ever since though, I have kept my eyes open, and this is the weird part. No matter where I am in America (and I travel quite a bit giving those little twenty-minute conference spiels that pass for scholarship these days), when I am in someone's kitchen, I find a copy of one of my poems on the icebox. Sometimes they are taped, but usually they are held fast by little magnets of all sizes and shapes.

How about that.

6. "Doesn't It Make You Wonder?"

I didn't believe it at first. Who would? I guess I expected my friends and colleagues to value my work, so when I found my poems hanging on their iceboxes next to their kid's finger paintings, I shrugged it off. "It's not like I'm famous or anything," I told my wife. "Doesn't it make you wonder?" she asked one night returning from a regional meeting of the AAUW where she'd seen one of my poems "right there on the door of the refrigerator of a woman I didn't even know and who, I am quite sure, has never heard of you."

It did make me wonder. I called some of my friends and got them and their families involved in the case. A few weeks later, a graduate school buddy called and said his son saw nineteen poems (all mine) on the doors of the cold storage lockers at La Maison de Paris in Atlanta where he is in his third term of cooking school. Then a former colleague, who now lives in Las Vegas, called. She has all sorts of video equipment, and she was going through a tape she'd taken off PBS of a White House tour. When she slowed down a panning shot of the kitchen, clear as a bell in one frame was one of my poems right there on the President's icebox.

How about that!

7. An Attempted Solution

After I had documented a thousand or so confirmed icebox poetry sightings, I sent my manuscript back to Natu Brave, Editor with a list of the names and addresses of the owners of iceboxes in America upon whose doors my poetry could be found. He was not impressed. He sent the manuscript back (in my S.A.S.E.) with the following note.

> Dear James Perkins:
>
> You are wasting your time as a poet. You are either nuts or one of the very best fabulists writing today. Please do not write to this press again. Any further correspondence from you will be forwarded promptly to our legal department. I mean it.
>
> Sincerely,
> Natu Brave, Editor

8. Plan B

How about that! Getting poetry published in America is a war of attrition or a crapshoot. When my manuscript came back that second time, my wife asked, "What are you going to do now?"

"I don't know. Look for another publisher, I guess."

"Why don't you ask him if he has one of your poems on his refrigerator?"

"Ask who?"

"Your publisher. What's his name?"

"Natu Brave, Editor."

"Ask him."

"He threatened me with legal action if I ever write to him again."

"So call."

I didn't think it would work. I didn't think I would ever get through to Natu Brave, Editor by phone. I've been hung up in those messaging systems at publishers for hours just trying to get a few examination copies to sell for beer money. But I heard, "If you know your party's last name, press the pound sign and enter it now." Natu Brave, Editor answered on the second ring.

"Natu Brave, Editor. How may I help you?"

"Just answer me this Natu. Do you have a copy of one of my poems on your icebox?"

"That's you, isn't it, Perkins? I told you not to call me."

"You told me not to write. Now just answer the question. By the way I'm taping this call."

"So am I, and I'm going to send a copy straight to Legal. Three is the answer. I have three of them. I don't know where they came from. I don't know how they got there. But when you came up with this silly crap, I went home and looked at my refrigerator door. You know that is something most people don't do?"

"You mean most `sane people,' don't you?"

"Read into it what you will. At any rate there are three of your poems on my refrigerator door, two photocopies and one that appears to be an original typescript."

"Wow that must be an old one. I've used a laser jet printer for the past ten years."

"None of these were in your manuscript. They are all quite good. I know I would have remembered them."

"I've written over eight hundred poems. I had to choose. Wait a minute. I'm loosing my thread here. What I want to know is does the fact that you have my poetry on your icebox alter your decision about publishing my "collected works?"

"I'm afraid not, my boy. A fist full of swallows does not make a spring. I'll tell you what I will do though. I'll put the marketing guys on this refrigerator thing, first thing Monday."

"Then you don't think I'm nuts?"

"Of course you're nuts, but I never let a thing like that stand in the way of making money."

9. The Marketing Guys

Have I mentioned that my wife is wonderful? She is supportive, and she comes up with the best ideas. I would have never thought to call Natu Brave, Editor.

About three weeks after my phone call to Natu Brave, Editor, we got a next-day mail pouch containing a stamped, return, check-off card that the marketing guys had dreamed up. It had all the usual demographic stuff:

- Name
- Address (with Zip Code)
- Age
- Sex
- Income
- Number of Dependents
- Education Level

Then it got down to a bunch of marketing-based questions like, number of credit cards you use, magazines you read per month, number of books you buy per year, internet service, number of movies you rent per month, all the usual stuff, like I said.

Then I saw it about half way down the card

#23Do you have poetry on your refrigerator door? ☐ Yes ☐ No
(If your answer to #23 is "No" go on to question #25)
#24Whose poetry is it?

☐ Maya Angelou

☐ Dylan Thomas
☐ Walt Whitman
☐ James Perkins
☐ Theodore Roethke
☐ James Wright
☐ Lyn Lifshin
☐ (Other)____________

Then the survey went on to ask about liquor consumption (number of liters per month), CD buying habits, clothes budget, vacation plans, etc. As an incentive to fill in the card, everyone who returned it by the deadline would be sent a free ticket for the multi-state Powerball Lottery drawing.

My wife and I didn't fill it out, but I was very pleased to see that the marketing guys were on the case. It seemed obvious to me that their scientific survey would confirm the anecdotal evidence that my network of friends had amassed and that shortly I would have my *Collected Poems* published by Natu Brave, Editor. How about that!

10. Report

Since part of my accommodation with the modern world involves teaching courses in public relations and advertising to bright young people whose parents are afraid that poetry is no longer "relevant," I was aware that it would take some time for the marketing guys to get their replies back, tabulate the results, test them for validity and significance and get a report to Natu Brave, Editor.

Two months later I got the following letter.

Dear James Perkins:

The Marketing Division reports that (based on a random sample of 120,000 homes in 20 key states) your poetry achieved a 93% penetration. To put that in layman's terms, more than 9 out of every 10 respondents (and let me say here that we had a remarkable 67% response rate on this questionnaire) reported that they have one (or more) of your poems on their refrigerator.

As a publisher, a successful one, for nearly twenty years, I know it would be pointless to try to enter a market that is already nearly saturated with the product. To put that in layman's terms, nearly everyone in America already has one of your poems hanging on the refrigerator door.

I think you can see it would be anybody's guess as to whether or not they would ever want another poem by you. So I am still not interested in publishing your "collected poems."

However, I do see a fine merchandising spin-off in all this research. If you will accept the enclosed check for $50,000 as an advance against our usual 15% merchandising royalty (This is considerably more than you would make off the publication of your "collected poems." We at the press never give an advance on a poetry book) and sign the enclosed contract permitting us to reproduce your signature and likeness, we are prepared to manufacture and distribute nationwide **James A. Perkins Magnetized Refrigerator Poetry Frames** with your picture and signature on them.

Sincerely,

Natu Brave, Editor

11. Satisfaction

How about that!

About the Author

James Ashbrook Perkins taught English and public relations at Westminster College, New Wilmington, Pennsylvania. He holds a B.A. from Centre College, an M.A. from Miami University, and a Ph.D. from The University of Tennessee.

Although his major interest is poetry, he has written scripts for radio, television, and films, published a number of short stories, and even tried his hand at what he feels is the dullest form of prose, the scholarly article. His books include: *The Amish: 2 Perceptions* 1976 (poetry); *Billy the Kid, Chicken Gizzards and Other Tale,* 1977 (short stories); *The Woodcarver,* 1978 (poetry); *The Amish: 2 Perceptions 2,* 1981 (poetry); *Snakes, Butterbeans and the Discovery of Electricity* 1990; reprinted 2003 (short stories); *Southern Writers at Century's End,* 1997 (edited criticism with Jeffrey Folks); *Robert Penn Warren's* All the King's Men*: Three Stage Versions,* 2000 (edition with James A. Grimshaw); *For the Record: A Robert Drake Reader,* 2001 (edited collection with Randy Hendricks); *Brother Enemy: Poems of the Korean War,* 2002 (edited translation in collaboration with Suh Ji-Moon); *The Cass Mastern Material: the Core of Robert Penn Warren's* All the King's Men (2005); *David Madden: A Writer for All Genres,* 2006 (edited collection with Randy Hendricks); *The Selected Letters of Robert Penn Warren* (edited with Randy Hendricks and William Bedford Clark), volume 3, 2006; volume 4, 2008; volume 5, 2011; volume 6, forthcoming.

In 1971 he was awarded the Mississippi Arts Festival Senior Poetry Award for his series "Maps and Highways." In 1975 and 1976 he was named Canaras Fellow in Poetry for the St. Lawrence University Writer's Conference. He was awarded a place in NEH Summer Seminars four times: at Princeton University, 1977; at New York University in 1981; at New York University in 1985; and at Yale University in 1989. In 1986 he was the Henderson Lecturer at Westminster College. In 1998 he was a Senior Fulbright Visiting Professor at Seoul National University in Korea. In 2003 he was the first McCandless Fellow at Westminster College. In 2005 he was named a Kentucky Colonel for his work in obtaining a United States postage stamp in honor of the centenary of Robert Penn Warren's birth. In 2006 he received a Watto Award and was named a Distinguished Faculty Member by Westminster College. In 2008, Perkins retired from teaching and was named Professor *Emeritus.*